A Plant

by Leslie Mills
illustrated by Kathi Ember

Practice Decodable 14

McGraw Hill Education

Bothell, WA • Chicago, IL • Columbus, OH • New York, NY

MHEonline.com

Send all inquiries to:
McGraw-Hill Education
8787 Orion Place
Columbus, OH 43240

ISBN: 978-0-02-132621-1
MHID: 0-02-132621-5

Printed in the United States of America.

7 8 9 CTM 23

Pal sits still in plants.

Lil can see Pal sit.

Lil can stand and slap.

Lil slips! A plant tilts.

A plant tips! Did it spill?

Sad Lil is damp!